Sad Kitsch

a poetry collection

Dawn E. Dagger

Contents

From the Pages of

Literature

Cutting Hair

Levanine's hair—

A holy proclamation

Cut by a pirate.

A decree of her new life.

A freeing of her past as a servant.

Noh'ri cuts her hair—

Takes dull shears

And hacks away at the dark curls

As tears fall down her cheeks.

A spite against the rules,

A proclamation that god

And man

No longer own her.

Inez cuts her hair—

Begging, sobbing

Chest heaving

For her goddess

To save her friends.

A holy sacrifice of her beauty;

Of the thing she tended to

Just for the divine—

A proclamation of desperation,

Imploring them to help.

As a child, I watched Mulan cut her hair—

To hide who she was,

To protect those she loved.

But, I always thought

Instead

That cutting her hair

Revealed her true identity,

All that was hiding.

I cut my hair—

A donation, for those who need it more.

But I am secretly hoping

That it will be short.

That I will be freed from the imprisonment

Of others' thoughts

About my beauty and femininity

And 'pretty hair.'

A proclamation that I am not—

Her—

Who they think I am.

What am I escaping from?

I am not sure.

But Levanine from her servanthood

And Noh'ri from her possession at the hands of men

And Inez from death.

The hair falls away,

Misshapen piles on the wooden floorboards—

Something that tastes like escape.

Hall of Mirrors

I write stories—

Characters seeking to be

Reunited

With those they were separated from.

Searching

For familiar faces.

Longing

For the embrace of their loves.

I wonder each time

Their eyes search the crowd

And their soul reaches out into

The universe for connection

What part of myself

It is spurred by.

So many of these characters

Like a scene in a movie

Looking into the mirrors all around

Seeking a face

Not their own.

But I am not seeking

The visage of someone else

I look into the fractals

The twisting light and shifting colors

Seeking something different.

Myself.

I long to reunite

With my long lost friend,

My passionate counterpart.

I seek to find

Me.

Maladaptive Daydreaming

Venice, Italy

Or the islands of Greece

Seem no more real

Than 221 Baker St,

Where Sherlock Holmes works

With John Watson.

Both unobtainable.

Both in media,

Never for my hands

To reach through the screen

And touch.

Paris is a place in songs

And movies—

The Eiffel Tower like

The unicorn print

Of a child's wallpaper.

Where the Soul is Housed

Hell is located in London.

And I think the soul is located—

Not near the heart, protected by the ribcage,

But, rather—in the wrists.

Soft, pale flesh

Aching

To have the vibrant life

Torn from underneath—

Like a vein

From a shrimp.

Exposed to the elements,

So close to the surface.

Always on the verge

Of being 'freed.'

As Poets of Old

This book is nothing more

Than a collection

Reminding me

That I am the same

As the poets of old.

I sit

And I pout

And I dig my feet into the dirt.

I gasp for air,

Trying to be thankful.

But the cold chill—

Icicles under my rib bones

And that same dreadful feeling

As the air between the pages

Of a gothic horror—

Prevents me

From being anything more

Than a tower of cards

On the verge of collapse.

Perhaps I am a structure

Of painted tarot cards.

Perhaps if I were

To finally fall apart

And crumble,

Scatter across the ground

It would tell my future.

The Fool,

The Hanged Man,

The Empress,

The Chariot.

The same melancholy

That gripped Sylvia Plath

– *"I am terrified by this dark thing that sleeps in me."*

And Edger Allen Poe

– *"I felt that I breathed an atmosphere of sorrow."*

And Franz Kafka

– *"I cannot make you understand. I cannot make anyone understand what is happening inside me. I cannot even explain it to myself."*

Grips me.

And I fear that,

Just as it never let them be,

It shall never

Let me free, either.

A Muzzle Filled with

Blood

"That is Not What Happened"

To-be-signed contracts

And editing gigs—

Things I've dreamed of.

Too much work to do.

A blessing.

And yet I feel a different pressure

To print and take pictures of

All that is happening.

To suddenly be a historian.

So that in 10 years

I am not told

My memory is failing me

And "That

is not what happened."

0325

I had hoped that evil

Was calculated and organized—

Suits around a mahogany table

Planning their destruction,

With foresight and

(god forbid I call it)

Elegance.

But I have discovered that evil

Is a secondary thought

In a text message.

Talk of bombs dropping,

Of killing human beings with souls—

Like a bunch of frat boys

In a locker room

Texting about the waitress at *Hooters*.

Slaughtered Children

You do not see

Children

as children.

You have

no faith

in their

Purity and Goodness.

All

are Evil

by nature.

You do not

see

their Innocence.

You do not notice

their soft hands—

Clean

and Bloodless.

No,

they are future soldiers.

They are born

either

Correct:

on your side

a companion to your cause.

or

they are born

Wrong:

Defective,

Enemies.

I cannot imagine

looking upon

a poppy field,

seeing only blood

and none

of the delicate petals.

I cannot imagine

seeing the stars

and wishing

that they were

Extinguished,

simply because

You do not own

the night sky.

110520242

Traded away

For a goat.

Mesopotamian tribes;

Old ways, long thought

Barbaric.

My body composed of cuts of precious meat.

I possess eggs,

So I am traded for eggs.

More people than I can count

Have decided

That I am a bride

And the dowry is milk.

Turkish Delight

Edmund traded his siblings

For Turkish Delight.

Sweet, pleasant treats

Benefitting only him.

They did not taste of blood

Or betrayal

But instead sweet jam

And snowy, white powder.

He looked in the eyes of a stranger

Who commanded respect—

Whose actions spoke louder

Than her soft, glacier words.

He trusted her

And wrapped his trembling fist around

The treats she offered.

The Bear

The stranger or the strange bear?

The strange bear

Does not have words

To tell me sweetly

That I've earned it

As he kills me—

Though I might have.

He is a bear after all.

I am the stranger

In his world.

The strange bear is predictable—

As long as I don't

Touch his things

He won't touch me.

I understand the nature of the bear—

Territorial,

Seeking fat to feed his hibernation.

And though the stranger may call me 'fat'

The strange bear knows

That salmon is better

Worth more effort.

The strange bear

With bared teeth

And bared claws

Is a stranger to the numbers

180 in 200 years *(the total number of bear-related deaths)*

89,000 in 2022 *(the total number of femicide victims)*

1 in 5 *(the number of women who have suffered completed or attempted sexual assault).*

And if my blood

Were spilled

On the forest floor

By the strange bear

It would be a tragedy.

My death

Would have a period;

Not a question mark.

The Language of Men

I'll speak in numbers—

For poetry is too emotional,

And words are, *like*, too imprecise,

And other languages are a threat,

And the way my soft, pink mouth moves

Makes you want to grab me

And harm me.

For how dare I try to speak——

Pressing words past my breasts?

I will speak in numbers,

The language of men—

So precise,

So factual.

Perhaps it is numbers,

The language of your own,

That will 'suade you

To hear me.

But facts are only facts if you state them.

And numbers are only numbers if you like them.

And people are only people if you say so.

So I will tuck my numbers back under my tongue

And close my folio,

Unplug my flash drive.

And I will use poetry and the language of others

To pray

That one day you will meet Empathy

And that when you do

That she does not smite you

With her holy light.

Candles Melting on a
Birthday Cake

Smoldering Candlewicks

I set myself on fire

To warm those around me.

I light the match

And like a candle wick

Am set aflame.

I rage, I warm,

I burn out.

I pretend I am a phoenix

Who's glorious death

Is the harbinger

For good in others.

That from the ashes I

Will rise again

To repeat.

When, in reality,

The ashes pile up

And the candles continue

To burn out.

And I do not know

The room is getting dimmer

And will soon

Be dark.

House on Fire

I left you behind in a house on fire,

Because there was nothing left

Of me to burn.

I tried to fireproof the house.

I installed sprinkler systems

Flooded by my own tears.

Stamped out the flames to soot

With my bare palms.

Took out my bones to prop open windows

So smoke could escape

And you could breathe.

But there was nothing left

Of me.

A ghost with no voice and

No form.

My charred body—

Decorations on the walls.

I had to leave

Before I faded

With the smoke in the dark sky.

But I left you

In the smoldering skeleton

Of a house

On fire.

Love Me "Right"

I want you to reach through

Thorn covered brambles

With your bare hands

Just for a chance

To touch my heart.

I want you to hurt

All in an effort

To make up for the hurt

I've suffered.

I want you to ache

Because I ached.

I want love to feel

Bloody and raw,

Full of tears.

Perhaps then

I will believe

I was worth loving.

Thankfulness

The bad is tenfold

The goodness is quiet.

My car breaks

But the gig will cover the cost of producing a story.

The book will come out.

The debts pile up

A neat collection on the refrigerator.

A museum curation of my failures.

I clench my jaw, teeth cracking

With the force of my smile

And I grip onto optimism

And thankfulness

So tight

My nails bite into my flesh

And I bleed.

Thankfulness and optimism

Feels like being beaten.

I do not *want* to be thankful.

I want to be upset.

I want to be angry.

But it feels that if I dare not acknowledge

The glimmers of goodness

Then the skies themselves

Will reach out to punish me.

It's sickening

Like drinking castor oil.

But then things aren't as bad

As they seemed.

And I feel as if

I'm just insane.

Self & Harm

I want to tear asunder

My soft flesh

With my sharp, dog teeth.

To bite others

Instead of just whimper

Or growl, tail

Tucked between my legs.

I am too squeamish

For the sight of

Bright, red blood.

Others tell me

That this weakness

Is a strength.

To not bite

'Shows restraint'—

And other words

Meaning 'good.'

But to me it feels

Often like defeat.

Rolling belly up

In the cold mud

So the carrion birds

Can rip tendrils of my heart

From the curved inside

Of my rib bones.

Circus Animals

I am a caged lioness

Without teeth,

My bite taken

Long ago.

Too pathetic to look at

For too long.

Clinging to life,

Fueled by rage

And ideas

Of better times

And better things

I've never seen.

Icicles in Empty

Ribcages

Lost Autumn

I want to shake myself

And scream.

There is no joy.

I am safe.

I am lucky.

There is no joy.

I should not be like this.

So broken

And disassociated

That nothing is joyous.

Pumpkin picking and flannel shirts

Decorating and fall candles—

Things that once brought me joy.

More work.

I should not be like this.

I cannot stop.

Shower 1

Salt water

Of the ocean

I'll never meet[1]

Mingling

With the too hot

Water

Of the shower.

It's supposed to get better

Isn't it?

---

1. *I have since met the ocean and she was as beautiful and salty as I'd hoped*

So

Why isn't

It better?

I am overwhelmed by

The good things

I am a part of.

My wedding ring

Sits on the bathroom

Counter,

My husband

And two cats

Sleeping

In the next room.

And yet

All I feel

Is sharp, gnawing pain

And the dissociation

Of my soul

Fleeing

My body.

I've worked

So hard

To be better.

I thought

I was

Better.

But it's back again—

The aching

The black oil stains.

The shower doesn't wash

The black blood that oozes

From imaginary wounds

Down the drain.

I sit

In my own thunderstorm

Wondering

Why.

Shower 2

I feel like

A sickly Victorian wife:

Wrapped in a shawl

With gossamer skin

On a frail frame.

Cold, pale hands

Paper-thin constitution.

A doctor in corduroy pants

Would recommend

A visit to the country

Or a vacation

Beside the sea

To cure me

Of my ailments.

'Fresh country air'

Or beach sunlight

Would be

The prescription

For whatever mysterious

Illness

Plagues me.

Perhaps

This imaginary man

With his leather bag

May be right.

Perhaps the cure

Is warm sunshine

And fresh air

To evaporate

The clinging darkness

Of Winter.

Perhaps rest

Would soothe

My weary soul.

But I am not a Victorian wife

With a well-to-do husband.

I cannot pack up and ride to the beach

Or hide in the dark green hills.

So instead I'll make

A cup of tea

And imagine that my shower

Is a waterfall.

And I'll fantasize

That my depression

Does not

Devour the goodness

Around me

Leaving me

Empty.

Frail.

Eternity

Sisyphus's boulder.

An ouroboros.

Sisyphus's boulder *in* an ouroboros.

Now there's an image.

Maybe it should be

The cover of this book.

Looping circles.

Nothing changes.

My rage has worn away.

Years have eroded the spite.

Now too does my optimism.

I want to spit,

Things do not get better.

Things do not change.

But instead

I'll bite my tongue until it bleeds.

The heavy taste of metal will remind me

That my words affect other people.

And lest I shove the tail of the snake

Into his fanged mouth,

I should simply keep silent.

Marrying Better Than Yourself

He is not religious.

A 6-hour drive

To a church in another state

To watch his niece

Be baptized.

A journey I would not be willing to make—

Even religious.

Too far.

But he does that.

Gives of himself.

I cannot be bothered

Past a mild inconvenience.

Am I truly so tired

That I cannot even fathom

Such an inconvenience

For the sake of another?

Perhaps he is better than I.

But I am tired.

Cold Chill

October,

like a bullet train,

sped past,

obscuring my view of what was on the other side of the tracks...

hope.

Things I've Inherited

The Curse of Montana

"I need a new life."

I dream of *Gone Girl.*

I cut off my hair.

Hop in a car,

Change my phone number,

Drive to Montana.

But my car is a debt

And I have $12.73.

Not even money for gas

To get to Montana.

I dream of trees and mountains.

Is it my dream?

Or is the demon that flowed through

My parents' veins

Flowing through mine too?

It was always Montana.

Crowded rooms and quarters in 5-gallon water jugs.

I dream of starting new.

I dream of someplace else.

I am safe. I am lucky.

And yet,

Driving home, all I can think of

Is how I would escape.

Childbearing

I barely know

Who

I am.

How can I

Rescind my youth

To those

Who don't

Know themselves

Either?

How

Can I guide

When I'm

Still

Finding the path

Myself?

I had

No youth—

For the burden

Of being

The eldest daughter,

The older sister,

The mother,

The father

Was mine to carry.

So many years

Of sacrifices

And changing diapers,

Of teaching

And reprimanding.

How could anyone

Ask me

To do it

Again?

Diagnosis

My greatest fear

Realized

No longer terrifying—

Simply…

Numbing.

A Pill in the Morning, a Pill at Night

> *September 10, 2022*
> **Respectfully, baseline existence needs to be less exhausting.**

September 10th

Years later

It hasn't changed.

Doctor's visits—

Things I thought stayed

As tragedies for others

And stories in books.

The doctor says, 'don't you know that you need to
visit endocrinology once a year?'

That is three doctors a year now.

Add dentist visits

And a trip to the eye doctor

The list seems endless.

I don't.

The doctor says, 'you need to take the pills again.'

I've been off it.

I felt okay.

The nightmares stopped.

Why?

The doctor says, 'you'll get cancer. You need to get your hormones under control.'

That means the nightmares will start again.

A pill in the morning. A pill at night.

For how long?

Indefinitely.

Indefinitely is eternity.

The rest of my life.

A pill in the morning. A pill at night.

The worst part

Is that nothing I do

Will *fix* the problems.

There is not an end goal.

A finish line.

There is simply manning the ramparts.

Not so it gets *better*

But so it doesn't get *worse*.

A pill in the morning. A pill at night.

Sisyphus's boulder.

Night terrors so vibrant life feels unsafe

or cancer?

What a choice.

A pill in the morning. A pill at night.

Something A Bit Like Irony

I fish pennies

And dimes

Out of the cup holder

Of the car.

Their faces are sticky

With iced coffee—

Remnants of moments

Where I felt rich.

I clutch them in my palm

Take them inside.

"Paris," I say,

Dropping them into the bank

On the bookshelf.

I set aside the quarters

For laundry.

Dimes and pennies

Chink, chink, chink.

I'll go to Paris.

I feel good.

Life has been good.

And then that night

My computer breaks.

And the pennies and dimes

Won't cover that.

And they won't cover Paris.

Why try?

The change will stay

In the cupholder,

Ready to be scrounged

For when $2.98

Is too much for my debit card

Once again.

When I Was Born
I Did Not Cry

When i was born

i gasped

With wonder

At the world,

i have been told.

i did not cry.

Instead, i sucked in

The beauty

Of existence.

But i feel

That i was born

With a dark pit

Inside of me.

i feel as if

That want

For death

Was sewn into

The cloth

That made me.

Is Life This Hard for Other People?

"Is life this hard for other people?"

I try to convince myself that it is.

It has to be.

Diagnosis after diagnosis confirms

That I am alone in my suffering.

That my life is so much harder than others.

Professionals hand me papers

And pitying looks

Telling me that I was built wrong.

Toy blocks askew and glued together in places

That just don't make sense.

But I try to convince myself that life

Is this hard for everyone else.

Because if I don't, then that means

That the misfortunes happen to me

And

That I suffer more than others

And

That there is no reason for it.

I feel no divine calling, no holy purity

In each daily struggle and moment of suffering.

I don't look back on moments, thinking how

They 'shaped' me as a more perfect creature.

Instead my memories are foggy patches

And I stare at pictures of myself, wondering if it's true

That I was once a little girl.

Because I often feel like

I was born this age, in this body, with this pain.

It seems eternal in both directions, never ending.

"It has to be."

I try to convince myself that it is.

Mobiles

Trauma—

A great equalizer.

The currency of status.

Those with the most trauma

Have the most currency—

Almost equal to those

Born to starlight and spoons.

Blood money

That projects

That I have struggled

Enough

To be worthy

Of good things.

Some are created

In goodness.

Security

A child

Born

Onto silk sheets

Staring

At a mobile

Of stars

Does not

Have to earn

The right

To touch

Those

Brilliant

Shining

Pieces.

But a child

Born

To darkness,

Staring

At angry faces,

Must somehow

Earn

The right

To reach

For those shining lights

Through blood

And tears.

Day of the Dead

Dias de los Muertos.

They have lists of names—

Short, distinct.

Lives punctuated by specific losses.

To celebrate

Day of the Dead

Would be to dig up the whole backyard.

Dead pets

And miscarried siblings

Hidden underneath the morning glories.

My list is a book—

Early memories are of funerals

And the rays of sunlight in my life

Being extinguished next to *Winnie the Pooh*

And a magnetic fish game.

To examine my losses

Is to break the drywall

And breathe in the asbestos.

To find skeletons in the closet.

I wonder what is life

If not a string of losses?

To Be Selfish

If I could be selfish—

I say.

Asking only for the things,

That others have.

Asking for simple dreams.

A child and a home.

If I could be selfish—

I'd have a little house

Where we could live

No longer displaced

Every season.

If I could be selfish—

I'd have a child

And not have to face

Blood

And single lines.

I preface with 'selfishness'

because asking for good things

seems like too much.

If I say *I want*

then I feel

as if it will all be taken from me.

If I could be selfish—

I'd like to be okay.

Sand and Deer Skulls

Young Deer

Cervus–

Antlers pointing to the sky,

Facing North,

Worshiping Polaris.

Round eyes glowing

With the secrets

That the universe whispers

Into their erect ears.

Cloven hooves

Like their master,

Who's name we dare

Not speak.

They feed of the fields

And of the forest.

With their blood

And the scent of their fear

Do they feed the Earth.

Faux innocence

Wrapped in soft, doe skin.

Mydas

Buildings crumble.

There is no childhood bedroom.

I dream of Notre Dame,

And Notre Dame burns.

All that I touch

All that I hold dear

Crumbles to dust.

A curse.

If Midas were doomed

To breathe in mothballs

And the aching decay

Of forgotten texts—

I am Midas.

The Silver Moon in the Quiet Sky

Hen & Chicks

Do you think my undying love,

My endless dedication to you—

When you have yet

To even exist—

Is enough to make God

Bend his will

In our favors?

Carbon Copy

I used to hope

My children

Would not be like me.

I hoped they

Would not be born

Full of rage

And hatred

And gnawing.

I hoped

That they would not

Live up to the words

Of those whom

Were supposed to

Love me:

"Your kids will be

Just like you

Some day—

And you'll

Understand

Why

I cannot

Like you."

Rude.

Aggressive.

Jabber-mouth.

Know-it-all.

Lazy.

But I hope now

That my children

Are just like me.

Full of love

For every creature that moves.

Kind.

Funny.

Smart.

Excited to voice

Every imaginative thought

And beautiful secret.

And I will tell them:

"I like you.

And I love you."

A New Favorite Song

The Fieldmouse

She ruined

A box

Of Spring things.

Sentimental

Pastel pink and

Sunshine yellow.

Important to me—

Gifts and reminders

Of better things.

The hole in the box

Is no one's fault.

Just as

The bitter Winter

Is neither mine

Nor

Hers.

She is so beautiful

I cannot even

Begrudge

Her actions.

For what is truer

Of Spring

Then the gentleness

And beauty

Of a small

Field mouse?

Daydreaming in Class

I want to write

Earth-shaking words

on the blank backs of tests

and tear-worthy phrases

on cola-stained napkins.

I want to carve greatness

in places not meant

for such things.

Instead, I write poetry

that's not quite "good"

and wonder if I've spelt

words like

"~~coniption~~" *conniption*

right.

Building a Future

My future will be a pyramid

Built on a foundation

Of stones

Cut by bloody, calloused hands.

Sweat

And tears

And the salt

Of suffering

Will place each block

Against the barren ground

Until slowly

But surely

The pyramid is built.

And it will stand

The test of time

And weather

And man's ignorance.

I will carve

A place in the world

With these bare hands

So that

Those who come after me

Will know their place

Effortlessly.

Aperture

How do people see me

So different

From how

I know

I am?

I can feel

The dark threads

The tangles

Of agony and rage

And to me

They dampen

The sunlight.

But perhaps

I am just

A cross stitch—

Needle work.

The front is

A beautiful picture,

Struggles

And love

Sewn

Into wildflowers and

Soft words.

The inside,

A tangle of threads—

Drops of blood

And tears.

The chaos

Does not ruin

The art.

Instead, it

Enhances it—

That such

Beauty

Could be

A result of

All those threads.

Perhaps

That

Is what others

See

In me.

My darkness

Does not

Diminish

My light.

It simply

Makes it

More

Beautiful.

Love & Life

Life sucks.

So, I'll love.

I'll be overflowing with it.

I'll tell everyone I know
That I love them.

I'll tell strangers
That their shirt
And their hair

And their smile

Are amazing.

And I hope that

The words

"You light up this world"

Are hidden

In every compliment.

I'll tell mothers

That their babies look

Just like them—

A kind lie.

I'll 'waste time'

Playing with my friends

And stay up all night

To talk about nonsense

That in ten years

Won't matter

But right now

Makes us feel

Connected.

I'll love so ruthlessly,

So unabashedly,

That it will flow

Like a mountain spring

From me—

Clean and pure

And endless.

And maybe life

Will continue to suck.

And maybe I won't

Make a difference.

But I could not care.

For I know

That the world

Has a little more love in it.

And those who I love

Feel a little more

Like life

Is worth living.

The 7th Deadly Sin

As a child

I was taught

That love

Was conditional.

It was a currency.

An indulgence.

Love is not free

Nor

Is it freely given.

And perhaps I am Gluttony,

Love dripping

From my fingers

And out

Of the corners of my mouth.

But I see no reason

To stop.

If my Deadly Sin

Is to love too much—

To drink words

Like honey,

To toss compliments

Like gold coins

To passersby,

To hold people,

As if they are fine china—

Then I will join the other six,

Take my place amongst Lust

And Greed,

Knowing I'd rather

Indulge in love

Then live piously

With a heart of brimstone.

Sad Kitsch

Maybe not all art

Has to be aesthetic.

Or beautiful.

Perhaps I don't need

Some grand meaning.

Maybe, sometimes,

I can just

Be a little ~~bitch~~ *kitsch*

About the Author

An avid reader and writer for as long as she can remember, Dawn Dagger is a free-spirited author who loves everything fantastical and caffeinated.

Dawn lives in Ohio, where she works as the marketing specialist for her local library. She enjoys adventuring with her husband, friends, and two cats.

She makes art at every opportunity she can. Whether cross stitching, designing websites, making commentary and gaming YouTube videos, teaching herself the piano, or something entirely new, she's always busy.

For more information or to connect with her, find Dawn and all of her books at:

Linktr.ee/dawndagger